Deafness

UNDERSTANDING
ILLNESS

Deafness

Elaine Landau

TWENTY-FIRST CENTURY BOOKS

A Division of Henry Holt and Company
New York

Twenty-First Century Books
A Division of Henry Holt and Company, Inc.
115 West 18th Street
New York, NY 10011

Henry Holt ® and colophon are trademarks of
Henry Holt and Company, Inc.
Publishers since 1866

Library of Congress Cataloging-in-Publication Data
Landau, Elaine.
Deafness / Elaine Landau. — 1st ed.
p. cm. — (Understanding illness)
Includes index.
1. Deafness—Juvenile literature. 2. Deaf—Juvenile literature.
[1. Deafness. 2. Physically handicapped.] I. Title. II Series: Landau,
Elaine. Understanding illness.
RF291.37.L36 1994
617.8—dc20   94-13843
                                                    CIP
                                                    AC

ISBN 0-8050-2993-1
First Edition 1994

Printed in the United States of America
All first editions are printed on acid-free paper ∞.
10 9 8 7 6 5 4 3 2 1

Photo Credits
pp. 11, 25: Phil Steinman/John Tracy Clinic; pp. 13, 17: Starkey
Laboratories; p. 19: Seimers Hearing Instruments, Inc.; p. 27: National
Library of Medicine; pp. 29, 32, 33: American School for the Deaf;
p. 30: The Jean Weingarten Peninsula School for the Deaf; p. 36: Ultratec,
Inc.; p. 37: National Captioning Institute; p. 40: The National Theater of
the Deaf; p. 47: Wide World Photos; p. 49: International Hearing Dog,
Inc.; p. 50: Highsmith Inc.; pp. 53, 54: Gallaudet University.

For Michael Brent Pearl

CONTENTS

CHAPTER ONE

Sounds of Silence: A Realm of Different Experiences

Sam was a deaf child born into a deaf family. As a young boy he was rarely lonely. His deaf brothers and sisters were fun to be with and Sam enjoyed spending time with them. Yet when he became a bit older, Sam noticed the little girl about his age who lived next door. After getting to know each other the children decided to play together occasionally. The girl was nice enough but Sam couldn't help seeing that there was something unusual about his new playmate.

It was immediately obvious to Sam that he couldn't communicate with her the way he did with his parents and siblings. He saw that it was hard for her to understand even the most obvious gestures. Feeling frustrated by the situation, Sam would simply point to things or pull her along with him when he wanted to go somewhere. Sometimes he wondered what was wrong with the girl next door. But as he wanted to continue their friendship, he learned to overlook her shortcomings.

Nevertheless at times his friend's behavior as well as that of her family completely baffled him. Once while they were playing at her house, the girl's mother approached them and began moving her mouth in a peculiar manner. Surprised that his friend understood what her parent was up to, Sam watched in amazement as the girl picked up a toy her mother had obviously been referring to and moved it.

More perplexed than ever, that night Sam asked his mother what was wrong with the neighbors. She told him that the people next door were "hearing" and didn't use sign language as his family did. Sam's mother further explained that they communicated with one another by "talking," which they used their mouths to do. Curious to know more about them, Sam asked if his friend and her family were the only people who did that. It was then for the first time that Sam learned that most people were "hearing" instead of the other way around.

That was a crucial moment in the boy's life. Still young enough to have largely remained surrounded by his deaf family and deaf family friends, he now found that they were not the typical American family he believed them to be. Instead of hearing people being the odd ones, one day he might be thought of as "different."

Tony was another deaf child, but unlike Sam he grew up in a hearing family. Tony had been born with the ability to hear but lost it when he was six as the result of a childhood illness. Looking back, Tony can't recall a specific moment at which he realized that he was deaf. Instead his awareness of it came gradually, as he describes here:

> I remember my parents worrying about me, and at some point everyone seemed concerned about my illness. It was at that point I felt changed, and when I thought about how I was changed my thought was: "I'm the only one like this." . . . I had a second cousin who was deaf,

*A young deaf child enjoys his birthday
party as much as hearing children do.*

but I decided I wasn't like her at all. She used her hands, she signed. I wasn't like her. I talked and I was like everyone else except I couldn't hear. . . .[1]

A third child—Jim—was a hard-of-hearing youth who, like Tony, was born into a hearing family. Unfortunately, Jim's hearing loss was not medically diagnosed until he was nearly seven years old. The problems he experienced due to missing much of what was said to him through the years were thought to have resulted from various other causes.

Prior to Jim's diagnosis, he never realized that people experienced sound differently. He noted, "I thought everyone lip-read but it always puzzled me that others seemed to lip-read better than I could."[2] After being fitted with a hearing aid Jim began to better understand things that had puzzled him for years.

Sadly Jim's story is not uncommon. At times many young people with hearing losses have gone undiagnosed for a large portion of their early lives. Although they may be desperately trying to make sense out of what's going on around them, often they are criticized for not paying attention or for failing to follow directions.

―――――――――

A daughter asks her 81-year-old mother, who has lost much of her hearing due to aging, whether or not she has on her hearing aid. When her mother answers no, the young woman responds, "Well, for heaven's sake, Mom, will you please put it on?"[3]

The daughter found her parent's hearing loss particularly difficult to deal with that day. She had been drawing up a shopping list and when she twice asked her mother whether or not she needed anything, the elderly woman hadn't replied. Chiding her mother for what she believed was carelessness, the daughter asked, "Why aren't you wearing it [the hearing aid] now? You know you miss a lot when you don't."

"No one understands," her mother replied. "My

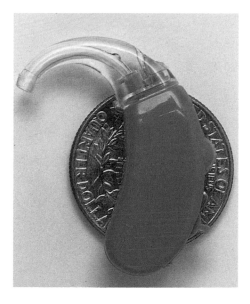

Some devices to help people hear are not very noticeable. The hearing aid shown here is about the size of a quarter

hearing aid brings your voice closer but it also brings me the sound of the faucet drip in the kitchen fifteen feet away, the whistle of the teakettle, the bubbling of the coffee percolator, even the bark of the neighbor's dog down the block. How would you like it if you had to listen to all that hullabaloo?"

While the details of each these stories differ, these individuals are actually more alike than they are different. Each is representative of countless others who have shared similar experiences. All involve either deaf or hard-of-hearing people living in a world where hearing is taken for granted. This book is about them.

CHAPTER
T W O

Causes

What causes deafness? Why are some babies born able to hear and others not? There are actually several answers to these questions, but one important factor is heredity. At times childhood deafness may result from an inherited problem. This means that someone in the family had this condition, which was genetically passed on to the child.

About 90 percent of such hereditary cases involve a gene for recessive deafness. Generally a trait produced by a recessive gene does not appear unless both the father and mother of a child have the same recessive gene for it. Often this recessive gene has been passed on for a number of generations. If a carrier never has a child with a partner with the same recessive gene, deafness may not occur. However, the condition results in one in four offsprings of parents who unknowingly have the same recessive gene. Because there might not have been a deaf person on either side of the family for some time, such parents are often shocked and confused as to why their child cannot hear.

In addition to recessive genes there are numerous other genetic causes of deafness. Unfortunately, in about 50 percent of genetic deafness cases, medical problems besides hearing loss occur. These include eye disorders, skin and nail problems, mental retardation, kidney mal-functioning, and facial deformities.

Deafness may also be caused by factors that are not hereditary. Some of the leading causes of nonhereditary deafness are described below.

RUBELLA, OR GERMAN MEASLES, AFFECTING A FETUS

When rubella, or German measles, strikes an adult or child, the result is usually not very harmful. Its victims generally experience fever, a red rash, and some minor discomfort. However, if a pregnant woman contracts rubella, its effect on her unborn child can be devastating. Numerous deformities may occur as well as brain damage and deafness.

MENINGITIS

Meningitis, an inflammation of any of the three mem-branes of the brain and spinal cord often caused by infec-tion, is the leading cause of childhood deafness among school-age children. Thirty-eight percent of the children who survive meningitis are also left with other disabili-ties in addition to hearing loss.

PREMATURE BIRTHS

New medical advances have saved premature infants who could not have survived in the past. However, in instances in which the infants are extremely small, the children often have multiple handicaps. Hearing loss is frequently one of these. Four times as many deaf school-age children were born prematurely as those with normal hearing.

DEAFNESS DUE TO MEDICATION

The development of new and seemingly miraculous drugs has been a boon to countless ill individuals. But although these medications enable a person to recover, at times there are negative side effects. Unfortunately, about three out of every thousand people hospitalized become deaf as the result of their medication.

NOISE-RELATED DEAFNESS

In addition to irritability, digestive problems, and bio-chemical changes, exposure to excessive noise can cause hearing loss. This condition, known as tinnitus, or ring-ing of the ear, has been picked up in teens who've spent a good deal of time listening to loud hard-rock music. However, generally the loss is not total and does not appear until the individual reaches adulthood. Medical researchers predict that noise-related deafness will increase in the future. This may be partly due to pro-longed exposure to massive industrial equipment, huge trucks, and loud rock music.

AGE-RELATED DEAFNESS

Besides those noted here, there are numerous other causes of deafness. At times these may include typhoid, smallpox, vitamin deficiencies, cerebral palsy, and mul-

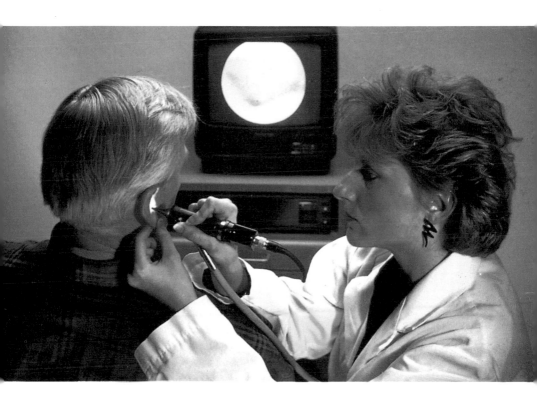

*Hearing tests help pinpoint the extent of a
person's hearing loss as he or she ages.*

tiple sclerosis. Age-related hearing loss among older
adults is still another common factor. The ear has sometimes been compared to a piece of machinery—it can
malfunction or wear out with time.

In age-related hearing loss, or presbycusis, older
adults lose some of their ability to capture and transmit
sound. Sooner or later most people experience it to some
degree. Heredity is frequently a factor in these cases.
People whose parents experienced hearing loss in old age

may do the same. Often it comes on gradually, and the person does not even realize it is happening. Older people who are not sure whether or not they've lost some of their hearing should ask themselves the following questions:

- Is it difficult for me to follow conversations when more than one person is speaking?
- Does my spouse or companion generally speak for me?
- Is communicating with others for extended periods exhausting?
- Do I sometimes answer other people's questions inappropriately?
- Do I frequently have to ask other people to repeat themselves?

A person who answers yes to one or more of these questions might want to see the family doctor. After examining the patient, the physician may send the patient to an ear specialist, or otologist. If the otologist determines that the hearing loss stems from a specific medical problem, he or she will treat the condition. However, if the patient's hearing loss is merely due to aging, the person will be sent to an audiologist.

A certified audiologist is someone trained to identify and determine the severity of the hearing loss. Audiologists test hearing using a device called a pure-tone audiometer, which focuses on sound pitches. Another test is having the patient repeat words, spoken by the audiologist, from a prepared list. In this case, a speech audiometer is used. The audiologist also devises

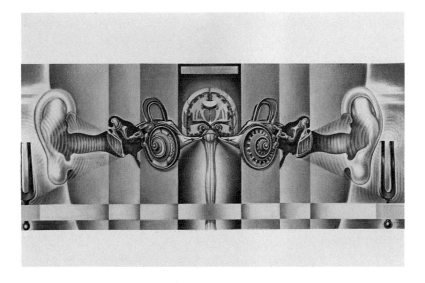

*This graphically shows the flow
of sound into the ears.*

ways to improve the patient's ability to hear, and may suggest a hearing aid or other listening device or system if he or she thinks it would be helpful.

Many older people find it particularly difficult to accept their hearing loss. Some may refuse to see an audiologist or even go to the doctor, insisting that nothing is wrong. When confronted about their hearing loss by friends and family members they'll make up an excuse, saying something like, "It wasn't that I couldn't hear that old bore. I just didn't feel like listening to the same stories he always tells."

In some cases these people may continue to deny that anything is wrong and feel too ashamed to talk about what's happening. Yet inside they may be aware that they don't hear as well as they once did. To preserve their self-image and pride, individuals may develop a set of behavior geared to keeping their secret. This may mean avoiding conversations in a crowded restaurant where people all around them are speaking and waiters and waitresses may be noisily serving a meal. They may carefully watch the faces of others and laugh when they laugh in case they miss the punch line to a joke. Instead of enjoying conversations with friends, they search for key words to grasp the gist of what's being said. They may also nod and smile more than they normally would to make the speaker think they've heard everything.

Pretending that nothing is wrong often also means contending with a variety of unflattering remarks. Depending on the situation, people losing their hearing may hear things like: "I know you're smart—your problem is that you live in your own world and don't listen to what you're told." or "You just asked me that five minutes ago. What's wrong with you?" or "Why didn't you answer the phone? I had to come in from the yard to get it, while you were in the room all along."

Undoubtedly telephone conversations frequently present special problems for people trying to disguise a hearing loss. Many individuals who always enjoyed exchanging news and views by phone come to dread the interaction they once looked forward to. If the connection is poor or if the caller mumbles, speaks rapidly, or speaks in a pitch that's particularly difficult for the other person to hear, the situation can be extremely frustrating for everyone involved.

One such woman who'd loved speaking to her grown daughter by phone described what frequently happens as follows:

"Now when I picked up the receiver and heard my daughter's cheery 'Hi Mom,' the lyrical quality of her voice brought a nervous quiver to my ears. I couldn't keep up with her pace and missed half of what she was saying. Sooner or later she would stop her chatter and ask a question. That habit floored me. Often I didn't know what she had been telling me. After a strained pause she would say, 'Didn't you hear me?'"[1]

In many instances mechanical aids and emotional support are available for those experiencing age-related hearing loss. However, these people must come to terms with what's happening to them before they can take advantage of these devices.

CHAPTER
THREE

Acceptance

Whether individuals are born deaf, become deaf as a child or adolescent, or lose their hearing later in life, they and their families must eventually accept the condition. If a baby is deaf at birth, the parents will generally be the first to deal with what had happened. Surprisingly in such cases the hearing loss is generally not diagnosed until these children are between one and three years of age.

At first parents may not suspect their child's problem since most infants can hear some sound. Children reacting to a loud noise such as a gunshot blast, thunder, or a foghorn may make their parents believe that they can hear. A baby's response to the vibrations of the mother or father walking across the floor can have the same effect.

But even though new parents may not be sure about their infant's hearing loss, they often sense that something is amiss. It's not uncommon for parents to later look back on the situation and say things like, "I thought it was strange that little Janie wasn't startled by the fireworks like the other babies," or "When the telephone rang during the baby's nap I was always afraid it would wake her, but it never did."

If the child's deafness isn't diagnosed early, related

problems often develop. As the baby fails to respond to them the way most babies would, the parents may wonder if the child is retarded or why the child never pays attention and finds it difficult to do what's expected. At times other family members or friends may suggest that the child is deaf or suffering from a serious medical problem. In any case the parents will have to eventually deal with having a deaf child. One mother who has actively worked to improve services for the deaf described how she first reacted to realizing that her child was deaf this way:

> My son Ronnie was jumping and yelling as he looked out the window with his back toward me. I called him but he didn't hear. When I reached his bed I was shouting and he still didn't respond. When he saw me he held out his arms. I realized that my beautiful, happy, and healthy baby was deaf. He could not hear his own voice so he yelled instead of cooing. . . . I can't remember much of the audiologist interview except that he told us, "Your son is deaf. He has nerve loss and no operation or hearing aid will make him hear." . . . My husband and I were totally unprepared. I had never known a deaf person. . . . Would my son . . . become an object of people's curiosity?[1]

Coping with the knowledge that a child is deaf can be difficult. However, the consequences of a delayed diagnosis or misdiagnosis are even worse. That's what happened to a couple who sensed that something was wrong with their unruly nine-month-old. They decided to have the child's hearing tested, and since one of their closest friends was an audiologist, the boy's parents brought him to the person they knew and trusted. Although the family friend assured the couple that the boy was fine, his mother still felt uneasy. She'd watched the child being tested and hadn't seen him respond the way she thought he should have.

Next the parents took their child to a neurologist who tested the boy with a tuning fork (a two-prong metal fork that, when struck, gives a fixed tone that is useful for tuning instruments and determining standard pitch) and diagnosed him as speech impaired. This led the mother and father to wondering if the problem had anything to do with how they'd raised him. So they saw a psychiatrist, who diagnosed the boy as having an early anxiety reaction to childhood, and the entire family went into therapy for six months. The parents and their older son felt better but the young boy still didn't respond to them appropriately.

It wasn't until he was three years old that his parents finally took the child to another audiologist. The second audiologist merely said, "This boy is profoundly deaf."[2]

Unfortunately, such experiences are not uncommon as nearly one-third of all deaf children are misdiagnosed at one time or another. This frequently occurs in situations in which the child does not see a specialist but instead a doctor who is not trained or is inexperienced in this area. In some cases physicians have performed crude tests such as dropping books on the floor behind a child to see if that child hears. Not realizing that the deaf child responded to the vibration rather than the noise, the physician might not think there is a problem.

*Once a deaf child is properly diagnosed, many
avenues are opened for both education and pleasure.*

In other cases deaf children have been misdiagnosed as being retarded, brain damaged, mentally ill, or having delayed speech. In one study a researcher identified more than 50 deaf individuals who'd been mistakenly placed in an institution for the mentally retarded. All had at least average or above average intelligence.

One of these children was a physician's daughter who had been placed in a home for the retarded and remained there for six years. After the girl was moved to a school for the deaf, she went on to graduate from high school, attend junior college, and complete her education at a prestigious art institute. A deaf boy found at the same institution transferred to a school for the deaf as well. He later graduated with honors from a university. These cases and others like them show the importance of ruling out deafness through thorough testing before arriving at a diagnosis.

At times parents who did not know what was wrong feel relieved to find that their son or daughter is deaf. But in any case both the parents and child will soon have to learn to live with the diagnosis in a society that places a high value on physical perfection. Societal attitudes regarding any disability often depend on a number of factors. Some of these are listed below.

THE INCONSPICUOUS DISABILITY

Disabilities that aren't immediately obvious are usually more likely to be misunderstood by the general public. Someone suffering from multiple sclerosis would not be expected to do needlepoint, but it's often thought that all deaf people can lip-read, and therefore could understand if they really tried. However, this is far from true.

Since deafness does not make a person appear physically disabled, some feel it's more acceptable to ridicule or make fun of deaf or hard-of-hearing individuals. Comedy skits involving elderly gentlemen with earhorns were unfortunately once common. There are also countless jokes about the supposedly humorous replies of deaf or hard-of-hearing people who misunderstood a question or mispronounced a word.

STEREOTYPES

Assumptions, lack of information, or stereotypes about a disability or medical concern frequently influence the way we treat one another. People who have never met a

*Deaf people were
often made fun
of in cartoons
and drawings.*

deaf person may nevertheless have some mistaken
notions about what they are like. Negatively referred to in
the past as "deaf and dumb" or "mute," deaf people may
still wrongly be thought of as stupid or antisocial by
some hearing individuals.

AGE

Studies show that teenagers are the most likely age group
to feel negatively about deaf people. Psychologists
believe that this is due to these young people's own inse-
curities. Being accepted is extremely important to many
teens and they often fear being different. Therefore a deaf
person or anyone who is somewhat different may be
more likely to become a target for ridicule and scorn.

FEAR OF THE UNKNOWN

At times people avoid others with disabilities because they are not sure how to act around them. When dealing with deaf people this anxiety may be focused on difficulties in communicating. Unfortunately, by maintaining this distance, hearing people may never learn to overcome their anxiety and work out effective ways of communicating with people who have hearing losses.

While growing up, deaf or hard-of-hearing individuals may not feel positive about themselves because of the negative attitudes they may encounter. Many deaf people agree that deafness is not so much a problem as the way society regards and treats it. A childhood marred by prejudice can take its toll not only on someone who is deaf, but on anybody's confidence.

Where and how deaf children are educated often has a powerful effect on their self-image and how they feel about other deaf and hard-of-hearing people. Deaf children may either attend a public school or a state residential educational facility. The concept of mainstreaming deaf children, or educating them along with hearing students in public schools, became extremely popular in the 1970s. In fact the Education for All Handicapped Children Act of 1975 mandated equal educational opportunities in public schools for children with disabilities. As parents were encouraged to send their deaf children to public schools, increasing numbers began to do so. In 1978, 33 percent of all deaf children in America were enrolled in public schools. By the late 1980s the number had risen to 53 percent.

Deaf children attending public schools might find

Various types of hearing devices enable deaf students to do well in school.

themselves in one of several different programs, depending on what's available in their area. Some are placed in classes with hearing children. If appropriate they use powerful hearing aids and are usually seated at the front of the room so that they can better hear the teacher. In other situations deaf students attend classes separately but share lunch periods, art classes, and recess with hearing children. However, it's been argued that deaf children are unable to fully take part in these activities due to communication problems.

Numerous schools have separate classes for deaf students in the early grades but mainstream them during junior and senior high school. Considering the negative

*At the Jean Weingarten Peninsula School
for the Deaf, children learn to speak and
are usually mainstreamed by first grade.*

stereotypes teens often hold regarding deaf individuals, these situations are sometimes difficult.

At time organizations representing the deaf, such as the National Association of the Deaf (NAD), have stressed that not all public schools are adequately prepared to educate deaf students. They emphasize that in some places deaf students are mainstreamed with only a minimum of services to meet their needs. Available statistics underscore their point. Unfortunately, the average deaf 17-year-old who has been mainstreamed at a public school only reads on a fourth-grade level. Without interpreters, tutors, and counselors, deaf students may eventually graduate with both a poor education and a tattered self-image.

Many deaf children instead attend state residential facilities for the deaf. Often they live at these institutions during the week and return home on the weekends to spend time with their families. These schools usually offer a wide range of services. Some even have special outreach programs through which instructors visit preschool deaf children at home to help them and their families learn social and communication skills prior to entering the classroom.

At times it's difficult for a child to be away from home for extended periods at a young age. One boy describes his feelings about his arrival at a residential school for the deaf: "For the first time I began to feel a sense of fear and foreboding. . . .We rode for a long time and then we stopped and found ourselves in front of an enormous building. . . . We walked into the building, and once inside I was immediately struck by a medicinal, institutional smell. This did not look like a hospital, or like any other building I had seen before. My mother, bent down toward me and said, 'This is where you will get your education. You will live here for a while. Don't worry, I will see you later.' Then she couldn't seem to say anymore. She hugged me quickly, gave me a kiss, and then, inexplicably, left."[3]

Yet some deaf people insist that there are distinct advantages to attending a residential school for the deaf.

*About half the students at the American
School for the Deaf live on campus.*

Often the staffs of these institutions include psychologists, social workers, audiologists, and teachers specifically trained to work with deaf students. Deaf children also frequently have their first opportunity to interact with other deaf young people in a host of social and athletic programs. They are also able to fully participate in leadership roles such as editor of the school newspaper, class president, et cetera. Many deaf people claim to have established meaningful and lasting friendships at these schools.

However, at one time there were some negative aspects. In the past, state residential facilities for deaf children placed a strong emphasis on speech rather than sign language. During the 1940s and 1950s children at these institutions were severely punished if they were

*Here a teacher at a school for the deaf
communicates with one of her students.*

caught using sign language instead of speaking. Teachers
were dismissed for doing the same. Therefore, young deaf
people often resorted to secretly using the silent language
they were comfortable with.

Despite continual practice many deaf people feel
they will never speak as intelligibly as hearing people
who grew up listening to those around them. When they
do talk, these deaf people often find themselves ridiculed
or pitied. As a result, some deaf people avoid communicating with hearing people. The following incident
shows what happened in one such situation:

A CHILDREN'S LIBRARIAN SPEAKS

I don't think I'll ever forget the first time I saw Anna. The fall school term had just begun and that afternoon our library's children's room teamed with young people. The staff delightedly welcomed back many of our old friends who'd been away for the summer and before the day was done we'd acquired an assortment of artwork and craft items they'd made for us.

Besides meeting and greeting young library users that day we were also extremely busy helping them find the necessary materials to complete their assignments. Everyone seemed to need a biography and before long only a few remained on the shelf. By about five o'clock the room finally cleared out. There were less than a handful of kids left and they had already found the books they wanted.

It was then that I noticed a tall, slim, dark-haired girl about twelve years old wandering through the aisles. I realized that she'd been there most of the afternoon but I didn't recall her speaking to anyone. She'd looked at the book spines and our display cases but she hadn't pulled any volumes from the shelf. As we were closing in about fifteen minutes I approached her to see if I could help her find something. But when she saw me coming toward her she moved away. Thinking that per-

haps she wanted to select her own books, I
retreated to my desk.

Ten minutes later we shut off the Xerox
machine and began flickering the lights to
remind our patrons that we were closing. It was
then that the girl's mother arrived to pick her
up. While the girl still stood at a distance her
mother came over and hurriedly blurted out,
"My daughter is deaf and came to the library
about three and a half hours ago looking for a
biography. She's embarrassed about the way she
sounds when she speaks and was afraid to ask
you to help her."

My heart sank. I thought about how she must
have felt all afternoon watching us help the
other young people. It was her library as much
as theirs, yet she must have felt like an outsider
looking in. Luckily we were still able to find a
biography she liked and before leaving she
smiled and said, "thank you." I didn't know
whether or not she lip-read, but hoping she did,
I answered, "You're welcome. Please come back
and see us again."

I hoped she'd come back and I knew that some-
how we'd communicate. Seeing her reaction
that day I imagined all the things she might
have felt excluded from. But information as
well as exciting adventures awaited her on our
shelves and I didn't want her to miss out on

Typing a telephone conversation is an efficient and easy way for deaf people to communicate.

that.

Fortunately the girl returned and she and the children's librarian developed an ongoing relationship. The librarian even eventually learned some sign language. They are positive proof that barriers can be successfully overcome when those involved are willing to try.

In recent years some exciting electronic developments have also brought deaf and hearing individuals closer as well as enhanced communication opportunities among deaf people themselves. These include the teletypewriter (TT or TTY), or telecommunication device for the deaf (TDD), through which telephone conversations

Here Robo Cop 2, *like numerous other movies, is shown with captions.*

are typed instead of spoken. There are a number of available options, such as having the message appear on a screen or receiving a printout of what's said. These devices permit hearing and deaf children to stay in touch with one another when apart.

Another helpful measure has been close-captioning decoders, which provide a printed display of the spoken dialogue and sound effects of a videotape or TV program. The captioning appears along the bottom of the screen during the show, allowing hearing and deaf individuals to watch TV together. In addition to such electronic advances numerous high schools now offer sign language as a foreign language option just as they do French, German, or Spanish.

Many hearing and deaf people share similar feelings, beliefs, and interests. Often they have a lot more in common than they supposed and should not be artificially separated because of physical differences.

CHAPTER
FOUR

Achievements

Despite the prejudice and obstacles they've faced throughout history many deaf people have made remarkable strides. In the eighteenth century the deaf population was larger than it is today since deafness was a frequent side effect of diseases such as the mumps, measles, meningitis, scarlet fever, and smallpox. In fact, there were so many deaf people in Paris during this period that a "deaf quarter" arose where deaf artisans and their families worked and lived.

By the nineteenth century the deaf community flourished in France. Newspapers for deaf people were published and purchased. Social and sporting events for deaf people were seasonal highlights that were eagerly anticipated. Numerous deaf writers and artists became extremely well-known and respected. Several deaf authors spent their lifetimes studying the history and achievements of deaf people and featuring such individuals in their work. There were so many outstanding deaf artists that a series of exhibitions called "Silent Salons" was held. It was during this period that the deaf French sculptor Felix Martin (1844-1916) became a member of the Legion of Honor—his country's highest civilian honor.

Yet unfortunately, this period of well-being for deaf people didn't last. Some hearing individuals, concerned that intermarriage between deaf people could produce deaf offspring, urged that laws be passed to prohibit such unions. Others tried to ban sign language instruction in an effort to force deaf people to speak and be more like people who hear. As these sentiments spread across Europe, repressive measures against the deaf also became commonplace in the United States. In 1942 more than 30 states passed laws permitting medical authorities to sterilize individuals considered "unfit" to reproduce. Deaf people were among these.

Sadly when this practice was legally challenged, the U.S. Supreme Court upheld the sterilization laws. The Court argued that if the country could ask soldiers to die defending it, deaf people and selected others could make "these lesser sacrifices in order to prevent our being swamped with incompetence." Accordingly by the mid-1940s over 36,000 individuals had been forcibly sterilized.

In time such measures were finally overturned. Yet even during that blatant period of ignorance about deaf people many still managed to excel. The deaf American sculptor Douglas Tilden (1860-1921) was acclaimed in his field, as was his student, impressionist painter and silent-movie actor Granville Redmond. A number of deaf actors had leading roles in silent movies and they often taught directors and hearing actors sign language. Charlie Chaplin, the famous comedic actor and director, used sign language in a number of his silent films.

Following World War II sign language and the concept of a distinct deaf culture gradually gained accep-

*The National Theater of the Deaf
provides an important forum
for talented deaf actors.*

tance. Deaf poets such as Dorothy Miles and, later, Dr. Clayton Valli used sign language to create a unique new form of poetry. And in 1967 the U.S. Department of Health, Education, and Welfare financed the National Theater of the Deaf (NTD) in Chester, Connecticut. This stage opportunity afforded deaf actors using sign language a chance to explore works concerning deaf people. Since then the theater company has been well received by the public as a window into the world of deaf people.

Within the broad scope of American achievement through the years, many deaf individuals have made valuable contributions. Early in our nation's history a young deaf man named Erastus Smith bravely served as a spy. Smith, who lost his hearing as the result of a childhood illness, was born in Dutchess County, New York, in 1789. When his family moved to the Southwest, the young man developed a love for the broad expanses of

Texas and often went out tracking game and hunting buffalo. As he traveled the territory, Smith became known as an outstanding trailblazer and was frequently sought out as a hunting scout and land surveyor.

However, before long Smith's life drastically changed. In 1821 Mexico won its independence from Spain and took over all of Texas. Although Smith had become a Mexican citizen when the Texas Revolution began in 1835, he was suspected of siding with his own people.

Smith had remained loyal yet a band of Mexican soldiers nevertheless arrived at his house to arrest him. He evaded his captors, but at that point Smith switched his allegiance. He soon became a key figure in the fight for Texas's independence. On various missions the experienced Texas scout led companies of men safely behind enemy lines. Smith was so successful that he was eventually promoted to captain and put in charge of his own company of men. His battle strategies proved crucial to Texas's victory and he was later honored for his contributions.

Deaf individuals have excelled in other areas as well. Among these was Luther Haden Taylor, an outstanding major-league baseball player. Taylor, who was born deaf in 1876, began playing baseball for the minor leagues after graduating with honors from the Kansas School for the Deaf. Soon thereafter his outstanding performance on the baseball field won him a spot in the major leagues with the New York Giants. Taylor did well as a Giant and was a favorite of the fans. He was extremely helpful in his team's winning baseball pennants in both 1904 and 1905.

Another outstanding talent from the deaf community is celebrity dancer Francis Woods (Esther Thomas, actual name). Born a premature baby without eardrums in 1907, Woods only weighed one and a half pounds. Although at first her doctors thought the tiny infant would not survive, Woods thrived and grew into an energetic athletic young woman. She attended the Ohio School for the Deaf where she was an outstanding player on the school's baseball team.

As a young woman Woods danced with her boyfriend, who later became her husband. While she was totally deaf and could not hear the music, she learned to dance to the vibrations coming from the dance floor. The couple practiced various steps in Woods's father's garage and won a number of local dance contests.

Known as "The Wonder Dancers," this husband and wife dance team became vaudeville stars. They later were a favorite act in major nightclubs and performed with a number of big-name bands. The Wonder Dancers enjoyed an exciting career, with fans in both the United States and Europe clamoring to see them perform. Even in their retirement years the Wonder Dancers continued to delight and entertain others. They gave dancing lessons to young children as well as performed for the elderly and handicapped in nursing homes. The couple was honored for their good works at an Ohio Governor's Award Banquet.

While Francis Woods entertained her fans with fancy footwork, another deaf American, Rhulin A. Thomas, took on daring challenges in the air as a pilot. Born on an Arkansas farm in 1910, Thomas completely lost his hearing due to a childhood illness. As an adult Thomas became a newspaper typesetter, but he pursued an exciting hobby as well. Whenever he had some spare time, the young man took flying lessons and eventually earned his pilot's license. Before long another dream came true for Thomas. After saving his money for years, he was finally able to buy his own plane.

Others might have been satisfied with all Rhulin A. Thomas accomplished. But the able pilot had still another important goal—he longed to be the first deaf person to fly solo across the continental United States. The trip would be particularly treacherous for Thomas since he couldn't hear the land-to-air radio communications vital to pilots. He would have no way of knowing when he'd fly into a storm until it might be too late.

Despite the risks, on October 26, 1947, he climbed into the cockpit of his plane to begin his 3,000 mile (4,800-kilometer) coast-to-coast flight. As might be expected, the journey was hardly problem-free. Thomas had to deal with frightful storms while flying over America's heartland. Once the weather conditions threw him so far off course that he ran out of gas. But he was soon on track again after making an emergency landing to refuel. On November 7, Rhulin A. Thomas safely arrived at his destination and made history.

At a White House ceremony on September 30, 1948, Thomas was awarded a gold medal engraved with the words "First Deaf Solo to Fly the Continent." Rhulin A. Thomas's achievement served to let the hearing world know that deaf people could overcome seemingly insurmountable obstacles both on land and in the air.

A number of deaf Americans have also made important strides in biochemistry and medicine. These include Donald L. Ballantyne, Sr., a brilliant medical researcher, who was a pioneer in the field of experimental surgery. Dr. Ballantyne earned a Ph.D. in biology and later specialized in devising plastic surgery techniques to help burn victims and other injured people. But perhaps one of his most exciting research projects entailed developing microsurgical techniques to reattach severed body parts. Microsurgery involves specially trained doctors using powerful microscopes to perform delicate operations. Ballantyne became so skilled in these procedures that he was dubbed "a master teacher" and became internationally known for his skill.

Still another deaf person who strove to enhance the lives of others was African-American Andrew Foster. Foster was born in 1925 in Birmingham, Alabama. As a boy he had spinal meningitis and was left completely deaf. After graduating from college, Foster moved to Washington, D.C., to work with other African-American deaf people. While living there he learned that in Africa there were more than 250,000 deaf people with only 12 schools for the deaf.[1]

Andrew Foster grew determined to go to Africa to teach deaf people as well as spread Christianity. To prepare for his mission, Foster earned a master's degree in education and studied ministry work at Seattle Pacific University. After a great deal of planning and fund-raising Foster began his work in Ghana. He established an ongoing mission center and school for the deaf there before extending his efforts to seven other African countries. Andrew Foster received numerous awards and honors for his work, including having been elected president of the Council for the Education and Welfare for the Deaf in Africa.

While Andrew Foster did a great deal for deaf people, National Football League (NFL) player Kenny Walker has served as an important role model in a different way.

Walker was the youngest of six African-American children born to a family in Crane, Texas. When he was two years old, he lost his hearing through a bout with spinal meningitis, making him the only deaf child in town. The boy coped well after learning to read lips and use sign language. Yet at times other children did not see past his deafness and left him out of activities. When they chose players for sports teams, Kenny Walker was usually picked last. However, after displaying his athletic ability in the gym or on the field, he'd be chosen first the following day.

Although the enterprising young man didn't even try out for football until his junior year of high school, before long he was a team star. A number of colleges tried to lure him to their campuses to play on their teams. But after considering the possibilities, Walker chose the University of Nebraska where he became a defensive tackle for the Nebraska Cornhuskers. Kenny Walker performed exceptionally both as an athlete and a student. Besides winning the cheers of those filling the university's stadium stands, he also earned a high B average as an art major.

Afterward Kenny Walker became the NFL's only nonhearing player when he signed up with the Denver Broncos. While Walker was on the football field, an interpreter helped relay play instructions to him through sign language. The skilled deaf player also read the defensive captain's lips for cues.

Kenny Walker has used his accomplishments to show society what deaf people are capable of as well as serve as a role model for other deaf individuals. As his interpreter said of him, "From day one he said, 'I think we can make an impact so let's.' He's savvy enough to use this to the benefit of those who could use a spokesman and a role model. We have opened the door for some deaf athletes, for example, that might not have opened if he had not chosen to let everything be known about his football career."[2]

Actress Marlee Matlin is still another deaf person who's made a difference. Matlin, who was born in the Chicago suburb of Morton Grove, lost her hearing when she was 18 months old as the result of an illness. Although adjusting to their daughter's hearing loss was difficult at first, the Matlin family learned to successfully cope. To enable them to communicate with her, Matlin's parents as well as her two brothers learned sign language.

Matlin's interest in acting began at a young age. As a child she acted with the Children's Theater for the Deaf in a nearby town. By the time she turned eight, the young girl had won leading roles in such productions as *The Wizard of Oz*, *Mary Poppins*, and *Peter Pan*.

However, Marlee Matlin caught the public's eye after playing the starring role in the movie *Children of a Lesser God*. The film is about a hearing teacher of deaf children who falls in love with a young deaf woman and their struggle to overcome their differences.

The movie's success meant more than just personal acclaim for Matlin. She hoped it might open doors for deaf actors and actresses to be cast in productions that aren't just about the problems faced by deaf people. But even after Matlin won an Academy Award for her performance in *Children of a Lesser God*, most people thought her career opportunities would still be severely limited.

Yet through her talent and determination the young

Marlee Matlin testified before the Senate committee on labor and human resources. She asked Congress to create a new institute for the deaf: "We want a home of our own," she said.

deaf actress proved them wrong. Since then Matlin has starred in the dramatic television series *Reasonable Doubts*, in which she plays a prosecuting attorney. While her character tackled challenging legal issues on the show, the fact that Matlin is deaf is merely incidental. It was just what the actress had wished for—a role relating the true capabilities of deaf people and their rightful role in society.

In addition to these well-known deaf people there are countless deaf individuals who've made valued contributions in both their personal and professional lives. There are deaf lawyers, doctors, dentists, writers, computer specialists, and teachers. In fact, there is almost no job deaf people do not currently have or cannot do.

CHAPTER
FIVE

The Deaf Community

A large number of deaf and hard-of-hearing people live in two worlds—the hearing community and the deaf community. The deaf community is made up of deaf and hard-of-hearing people who identify with other deaf individuals and share a common set of beliefs, values, and behaviors. The deaf community also includes family, friends, and others who can communicate easily with one another. Geographically, deaf communities exist in towns and cities throughout the country. Deaf people and those close to them get together to enjoy one another's company and take a break from the hearing world.

Unlike the hearing majority who view deafness as a medical problem or physical disability, the deaf community sees deafness from a cultural perspective. As the hearing child of deaf parents described their feelings, "[It's the] pride Deaf people have in their way of life: that it is good and right to be Deaf."[1]

Some deaf people refer to themselves as Deaf, with a capital *D*, in order to be identified as a distinct cultural group. When Congress considered establishing a new facility to research possible "cures" for deafness, some Deaf activists were against it. They argued that no one would think of changing a person's ethnic background

"Denver Dog," a hearing-ear dog, alerts a deaf mother to her child's crying.

and that deafness should be treated the same way. Underscoring that deafness must be viewed as merely a personal characteristic rather than a "disease," one deaf activist said, "If I had a bulldozer and a gun I would destroy all scientific experiments to cure deafness. If I could hear, I would probably take a pencil and make myself deaf again."[2]

An important characteristic of the deaf community is the use of American Sign Language (ASL). This form of communication was not always automatically taught to deaf children and not all deaf people are equally skilled in it. In fact, of the approximately 24 million people with hearing losses in the United States, only a small percentage use sign language. However, in recent years the deaf community has actively encouraged its use and acceptance. Many deaf people consider ASL their first language. They tend not to use speech among themselves but to communicate through ASL.

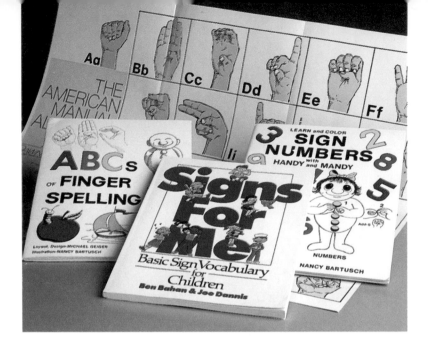

There are a large number of books and tools
available for teaching sign language to children.

Hearing people often evaluate a deaf person by the severity or degree of hearing loss. But within the deaf community, this is unimportant. It does not matter whether the individual can hear well enough to use a telephone. Instead, thinking of oneself as a deaf person and behaving like and identifying with other deaf people is what counts.

A sense of community among deaf people living in a given area is important in both forming friendships and taking part in social functions and events. At times groups of deaf people may be seen picnicking together or staying late at a party or restaurant, enjoying one another's company. In large metropolitan regions there may be several deaf clubs. Members of these groups meet regularly to hold parties, bowl, play cards, view captioned movies, and participate in sporting events as well as involve themselves in a broad array of other activities. Relaxing and sharing similar experiences is especially important to the deaf person, who may be the only deaf person at their workplace or in their apartment complex or neighborhood.

While the deaf community provides important social outlets, it functions in other vital ways as well. In recent years it has become a potent force in the movement for equality for deaf people. This was especially evident in the 1988 student protest at Gallaudet University—the only liberal arts university for deaf students in the world. Gallaudet, a federally chartered and funded institution, had long enjoyed a fine reputation. The school has been credited with turning out about 95 percent of the country's deaf professionals in such areas as education, law, and engineering.

Yet in March 1988 the esteemed center for learning turned into a hotbed of student outrage and unrest. Intense pressure from the student body and deaf community on the school's board of trustees to select a deaf person as the university's new president had gone unheeded. Instead, Gallaudet's board appointed Elizabeth Ann Zinser, a hearing person who did not know sign language and had no experience teaching the deaf.

Gallaudet students refused to accept the board's choice. They shut down classes for a week and marched to the White House in a silent protest that was loudly heard throughout the nation. Gates to the campus were blocked as the student leaders held rallies to insist that the university had a responsibility to set an example by appointing a qualified deaf person as its head. The protesters felt that anything less was an insult to the deaf community.

Many believed that the students and their supporters had a valid point. In Gallaudet's 124-year history, the school had never had a deaf or hard-of-hearing president. The protesters argued that this unstated policy reflected the offensive attitude that deaf people can't run their own affairs. As one student put it, "Prejudice is believing that hearing people have to take care of deaf people."[3] Her sentiments were echoed by Gary Olsen, a graduate of Gallaudet who was then the executive director of the National Association of the Deaf. Olsen viewed the Gallaudet controversy as follows: "It's not just a university issue. It's a national issue. Deaf people have been oppressed for too long."[4]

At first it appeared doubtful that the students would achieve their goal. Zinser, the newly appointed president, did not seem about to step down from her post. Instead, she firmly announced, "I am in charge." But others were determined to make her change her mind. These included Congressman David E. Bonier of Michigan, who was among the Gallaudet trustees in favor of appointing a deaf school president. Bonier suggested that if Zinser continued as president, Congress might not be as likely to increase federal funding to the school.

Bonier's feelings were shared by a number of elected officials. Seven members of the House of Representatives sent the Gallaudet board of trustees a letter voicing their disapproval of the board's choice for president. In addition, Vice President George Bush, along with several

Above: *Gallaudet University is devoted to higher education for deaf people.*

Left: *Many Gallaudet University graduates become successful professionals.*

*Dr. I. King Jordan conversing
with a deaf-and-blind student.*

would-be presidential candidates, sided with the students. Under the relentless pressure, Elizabeth Ann Zinser resigned, stating that she "didn't know we would have this level of conflict." Shortly afterward the Gallaudet board of trustees appointed a capable and extremely well-liked deaf president, Dr. I. King Jordan.

It was a monumental victory that reached far beyond the university campus. The deaf community had demanded equality and respect and America had listened and responded. As deaf people continue to pursue their rights, we can be certain they'll be heard from in the future.

E N D
NOTES

CHAPTER 1

1. Carol Padden and Tom Humphries, *Deaf in America: Voices from a Culture* (Cambridge, Mass.: Harvard University Press, 1988), 20.

2. Ibid.

3. Charlotte Himbler, *How to Survive Hearing Loss* (Washington, D.C.: Gallaudet Press, 1989), 2.

4. Ibid.

CHAPTER 2

1. Himbler, 21.

CHAPTER 3

1. McCay Vernon and Jean F. Andrews, *The Psychology of Deafness: Understanding Deaf and Hard of Hearing People* (New York: Longman, 1989), 92.

2. Ibid.

3. Padden and Humphries, 19.

CHAPTER 4

1. Robert Panara and John Panara, *Great Deaf Americans* (Silver Spring, Md.: T. J. Publishers, 1983), 96.

2. "Deaf All American Shares His Success On and

Off the Football Field with White Female Interpreter,"
Jet, January 21, 1991, 27.

CHAPTER 5

1. Sherman Wilcox ed., *American Deaf Culture: An Anthology* (Burtonville, Md.: Linstok Press, 1989), 11.

2. Towsend David, "Hearing Aid," *The New Republic*, September 2, 1988, 22.

3. David Brand, "This Is the Selma of the Deaf," *Time*, March 21, 1988, 65.

4. Jerry Adler, "Deaf Students Speak Out," *Newsweek*, March 21, 1988, 79.

GLOSSARY

audiologist—a person trained to determine the extent of a hearing loss. An audiologist will decide which type of hearing aid will help the patient.

German measles, or rubella—a disease that produces a rash, fever, and some minor discomfort. It is dangerous for a pregnant woman to contract the disease, as it may result in her unborn child having numerous health problems, often including deafness.

meningitis—an inflammation, often caused by infection, of any of the three layers that enclose the brain and spinal cord. It is the leading cause of childhood deafness among school-age children.

neurologist—a doctor who diagnoses and treats disorders of the nervous system

premature birth—occurs when the period of pregnancy is less than the full nine months. Premature babies can have numerous birth defects, including deafness or hearing loss.

presbycusis—age-related hearing loss

pure-tone audiometer—a device that helps to determine the severity of a hearing loss. An audiologist will place ear phones on the patient, through which certain pitches are transmitted to the patient through the pure-tone audiometer. The patient responds by raising his or her hand when the sounds are heard.

recessive deafness—results in the birth of a deaf child, where his or her "hearing" parents are carrying the same gene for a particular trait (in this case deafness) and that trait is passed on to the child

sign language—a method of communication in which hand gestures are used instead of speech

speech audiometer—a device used by audiologists to determine the severity of a hearing loss. The audiologist will place ear phones on the patient, then through the speech audiometer, he or she will read a word from the prepared list, which the patient then repeats. Many lists may be read to help the audiologist determine the exact type of hearing loss exhibited by the patient.

telecommunication device for the deaf (TDD), or tele-typewriter (TT or TTY)—one form of enabling a deaf person to communicate through the telephone in which conversations are typed

tinnitus—a ringing in the ears, often the result of being around too much noise

FURTHER READING

Bowe, Frank. *Equal Rights for Americans with Disabilities*. New York: Franklin Watts, 1992.

Kettelkamp, Larry. *High Tech for the Handicapped: New Ways to Hear, See, Talk, and Walk*. Cliffside, New Jersey: Enslow, 1991.

Krementz, Jill. *How It Feels to Live with a Physical Disability*. New York: Simon & Schuster, 1992.

Mango, Karen N. *Hearing Loss*. New York: Franklin Watts, 1991.

Parker, Steve. *The Ear and Hearing*. New York: Franklin Watts, 1991.

Tames, Richard. *Helen Keller*. New York: Franklin Watts, 1991.

Organizatons
Concerned with Deafness

Alexander Graham Bell Association for the Deaf
3417 Volta Pl. NW
Washington, D.C. 20007

American Auditory Society
1966 Inwood Rd.
Dallas, TX 75235

American Deafness and Rehabilitation Association
P.O. Box 251554
Little Rock, AR 72225

American Hearing Research Foundation
55 E. Washington St., Ste. 2022
Chicago, IL 60602

Children of Deaf Adults
P.O. Box 30715
Santa Barbara, CA 93130

Deafness Research Foundation
9 E. 38th St., 7th Fl.
New York, NY 10016

**Helen Keller National Center for
Deaf-Blind Youths and Adults**
111 Middle Neck Rd.
Sands Point, NY 11050

International Hearing Dog, Inc.
5901 E. 89th Ave.
Henderson, CO 80640

National Association of the Deaf
814 Thayer Ave.
Silver Spring, MD 20910

National Captioning Institute
5203 Leesburg Pike, Ste. 1500
Falls Church, VA 22041

National Center for Law and Deafness
Gallaudet University
800 Florida Ave. NE
Washington, DC 20002

National Foundation for Children's Hearing Education and Research
928 McLean Ave.
Yonkers, NY 10704

National Information Center on Deafness
Gallaudet University
800 Florida Ave. NE
Washington, D.C. 20002-3695

Self-Help for Hard of Hearing People
7800 Wisconsin Ave.
Bethesda, MD 20814

Telecommunication for the Deaf, Inc.,
8719 Colesville Rd., Ste. 300
Silver Spring, MD 20910

INDEX